# About the author

Pascale Lora Schyns is a Belgian writer and performer. She studied English and Dutch philology and literature at the University of Liège; acting at the Cours Florent (Paris, France) and at the Actors' Studio (Rome, Italy). A cancer survivor, she spends most of her time travelling all around the world. To discover new places and meet new people to reinvent them in her books is Pascale Lora Schyns' main occupation. She is the author of sixteen books published in French, English, and Spanish and facilitates creative writing workshops and dance therapy classes.

IF I WAS A MAN, I WOULD FALL IN LOVE

WITH GEORGE MICHAEL

# Pascale Lora Schyns

---

# IF I WAS A MAN, I WOULD FALL IN LOVE WITH GEORGE MICHAEL

Vanguard Press

# Dedication

To George and Melanie.

Airily bravely considering
how to creep along
to avoid controversy
to corrupt the discomfort

Evasively frenetically guessing
what could kill the lies
to liquefy levity
to pacify the rebellion

Prussian blue rainy self-love
Unburied altercations
Childish ailments
to allay his face alighted with joy
and accuse the cataclysm
of aggravating the aftermath of adultery.

A creaky cradle
a feared destiny
hallucination of glory

Handsome goblins where are you
to prevent the hilarious salamanders
from  injecting their unconsecrated saliva?

Winsome smile
Reborn recital
Prodigious magicians impressing honesty
legitimating trickery
flirting with their ecstasy

Cadenza duplicity of senses
Five-star happiness
Gorgeous harmony
Mellifluous masturbation
a precarious somnolence
for the mind aiming at loyalty.

Ubiquity seldom changes the lyrics of loss
consistent heredity envenoming the melody
the feeling of having love there
flash-forward of an older life
insomnia hammering in a bleeding heart

Is that eternity calling?

Remember the obedient sentinel
Taste the marvelous courtesan
Breath the astral futility
Challenge the diaphanous obscurity

Is that eternity calling
or just a blue movie
on the wide screen?

Naked and pallid
Gingerly offending the rhythm of death
throwing discredit on the ejaculating grace
giving away the gladness of self-hate

Lusty voices unevenly warbling memories
to lure debauch in a delicate trap
Changes exhausting the fantasy
Holograms blinking and dying
Silence of the vacuity

Worrisome frivolity
Insurrection maybe?
Don't measure tyranny
throw it to the sacrilege
Love needs no posology.

Haphazardly looking at crying eyes
and holding dominion over suffering lies
dysfunction eagerly desires to feel ferocity
to pay homage to the dead hearts

Imposture is the issue
Felicity is the heritage
Captive follies with glaring eyes
Hard-fought perversion
lashing the negligence of seduction

Listen  to the windswept high treason
          to the synchronized stupefaction
          to the quivering rhapsody
          to the monophonic lament

And never forget
          that you have been loved.

Intravenous relief for the soul
Careless whispers unmerciful venom
Write something new in my scrapbook
Something mythical something indecent

Insidious faith in a haughty merman
Melodious words exploring the limits
Bordering the prevalence of joy
Slicing the fecundity of disillusion

Don't dispirit the generosity of the gunshot
Fetal heartbeat in a hand puppet
daintily growing up out of time
to deliver hopeful and searing pains

When a lie is yours it becomes truth.

A rosebud seed for a new life
But the day is old and takes no risk
to avoid this feeling of evanescence
to embrace the subtle vicious circle
          of prosody
          of hegemony
          of docility
                         the red one


Put the incoherent words of happiness in jail
Free the full sentences
          the sad ones
          the pitiless ones
          the rusty ones


This is no sacrifice
This is not real love


Just a tangled tale hidden in a precious box.

Sunburned hands playing the grand piano
to endanger the coldness of your try

Essential deathbed for cynical thoughts
which damaged the fleshly malice of benevolence

Perilous slavery improvising with our certitude
blameless ignominy

Downhearted hopes
          where did you copulate?
          where are your pretensions?

Are they too credulous those who inhaled you?

You slipped into a marginal galaxy
and disappeared sotto voce
BUT DO YOU STILL HEAR ME?

Elegy of the ferocious thunderstorm
twinkling in our injured hearts

Listen to the breathy voice of change
Cast evil spirits out of our epitaph

Would our hymen be melodious
full of avid dizziness
or would it be a disruptive one?

I want it to be sweeter than a baklava
a divine cantata

I want it to cancel calumny
to espouse the cause of love
          merciless
          incestuous
          unconsidered
          but ours.

Impetuous commemoration of the inexistence
before the entr'acte brings diffidence

Sing me a tone poem
Hellfire preacher

I am pregnant with danger
I fear the wrath of their cancerous gods
serial killers of emotions
reducing fascination to rubble

O charming singer
don't cash me in the crossfire
don't disparage my truth
I am a joyful dreamer
        a joyless lover
        waiting for your audacious voice
        to heal the pain
        to tear the unbearable tattoo of death.

All-risks insurance
blown away by a Greek smile
Central locking
Ensconced in my favourite chair
wanting to go to a town

Where does he live?
Let me idle in the streets of his heaven-sent voice

Respect
Illusion reflecting vibration
Widowhood before the hour
Unnerving theorem
Stupefaction not mine never mine
          Lovelorn incandescence
          Pathetic ominous night bird
                  Kalispera.

Aimlessly yet foolhardy
deleting the letters of the gods
infringing the predictable references
      of comfort
      of boredom
      of disgrace

Wake up! You bystander

No more aloofness
No more harmony

Take the emerald of metamorphosis
Bring it to the guillotine
Inebriate your damned soul
      your pervading nostalgia
Preserve the swelling symphony of patience
Turbid thoughts in the middle of temptation
In flagrante delicto
thrown into the unconsidered mirror of shame
Wake up! Just for one more try.

To Laurie

Silky is her name
Silky was his name

Falling over a precipice of hazard
Glittering in memoriam

Highborn and peaceful survivor
You called a truce
to ramify indolence
and shoot the rapids of your emotions

bitter ones
corrosive sometimes
to decimate the evening stars
and fissure their hideous lethargy
before they reduce your heart to ashes.

Heaven takes a fiendish pleasure in mourning our victims
Evanescent threnody
Vaporous iridescence

Not even a lethal dose to lessen the pain
In vitro indiscretion
Let me see your handwriting
Is it furious sometimes?
Fornicating with the imbalance of a masterpiece
Hungrily looking for gold
the gold of first impulses

Fight them down
Don't let their flame lighten the mighty history of
paradigm.

Is disharmony the convergence of secret lines?
Horizontal ones
Dismantled ones

In the duskiness of chastity
eruptions of absence are caring for eclecticism

The eyes of grief have a faraway look

Lineal homicide to meet a new variation
Sharpshooter, try it again
Shoot the dog
No trial is requested
for breaking love into shivers.

Are jackals back in town?
Feverishly hunting innocence
devastating precocious and wild orchids
conceiving cruel whims
sinfully uglifying radiant smiles
Unquiet times for nonchalance

Are jackals back in our hearts?
Lascivious impure gamblers
singing in falsetto
to execute the doctrine of castration

Blacklisted anti-heroes
Shame on you
for censoring the brutal truth of contradiction
for relentlessly pursuing the shadow of injury

Jackals are back in eternity
to break brittle bones
                         Yours.

Alchemist, why don't you heal his pain,
his aptitude to behead compassion?

A double-edged hysteria lashes
his magnitude
his sparkling agony

Rescue him yesterday before it is too late
Deterrence will try to shred his honor
Ashamed for being loved
Barebacker
Barley sugar
Overdose of tears
Fortune-teller.

With bated breath
voices from below
were trying to carve
a new kind of distraction

Cruel and emotive games
intimate the lovers

Their inconsistency is over

Opalescent morning star
Perfection has no plural
Fusion becomes one
          one freedom
          one cosmos
          one resurrection

Why is it a crime
to be two in one
one in two?

Why does love live in a ghetto?

A clitoral confusion
devilishly
throws away the fluid of his coitus
Juicy groans hectically scavenge
in the dustbin of their chimera

Compulsive idealism dignifying frigidity

Languorous games
Fragments of ivory-white porcelain
Starless angels tarnished betrayal
condemned for now and forever
          to enforced silence
          to unsafe flattery
          only

Spring should have known
that death is nothing
but a chaotic eclipse.

To endure the frostiness of a once luscious smile
and without a word
turn one's back to celebrity
request a cease-fire
dance with history
and get a perfect erection

To hold one's soul riven by war
in consecrated ground
before crossing the limbo
effusively
to legitimate the last rites of polygamy

Unlocked creatures never search for emasculation

They crash
        or not.

Commitment felt abashed at gambling
apparently
Babel of voices buried
the effervescence of old-time serenity

Sleepy but unlined faces
exclaim their detachment
and blench at the sight of life
young and fresh life
baying at the moon

Bulimia by daylight
hungry for ephemerae
thirsty for a fondant heart

Gelatinous men wanting your sex
your sex only
when you desire nothing
but tenderness.

Bewitching heart pains
broke the bounds of marriage

Theirs not mine not ours
which do not exist

Crabby and dusty celebration
to electrocute Mary Queen of Scots
and let her decay in a mass grove
with nothing
but a feeling of nothingness

Libertine and shameless love
undulating
under the meanders of a funeral
that one
the one that frightened our dynasty of curious fears
our casteless governance
our licentious prestige

A fretful voice a father figure
are needed
to put a final point to underhand dealings.

Was that an agreement?
A kind of entertaining and bilingual firebreak
murmuring otherworldly perceptions?

Was that you?
Was that me?
Was that our paralytic voice
trying to satisfy swift and de facto orgasms?

Together apart
troubling bodies wanting nothing
but uterine and panoramic sex.

Every day spring and autumn alike
ethereal minds and bodies
foray in a forbidden way

Mesmerizing and venomous paths
leading to the nowhere of love

Vapid and boggy banquets
where gangbangs drink the soul of their emptiness
bereaved for not being able
of finding a blanket
to hide the lost battles
cringing in front of insipidity

Just what they feel
Just what they are
a mute and quavering old-fashioned voice.

Furthermore
        Furthermore
        he decided
        he defended  he did not
accept the doings
of feeble minded and under hypnosis pathfinders

Furthermore
        he vacillated
between terse and scenic landscapes of joy
        unreal joy

Maddening the inaccuracy
        of hale and hearty geometry
        of vanished hearts
        of broken souls
        of love
a word that never existed.

Is there any alternative to bareness
to a degrading flood of panic

A parenthesis
a glimpse
to deform the fateful history
of a maidenly love

to make overtures to coral red lips  easy to please ones

indecent exposure

tormented enthronement

a sprinkle of rain
just borrowed an expressionless frame.

Use a dildo
use a dildo
to remember I went
he used to tell him

Use a dildo
like a whirling dervish would do

a diagonal one
to destroy the verdict of abandon

a providential one
to amplify the effect of joy

a crucial one
to appease the contemptuous absence

One more try

If it does not work
If your soul is still scared
If you do not forget my flint heart
Maybe I shall come back.

A disappointing throat
even a tactful one
cannot discern the metronome
behind the footlights


        a gentle hint
        in the penumbra

        an overwhelming blink
        achromatic bribery


Chastity will die childless
                colorless
and failure will look witheringly
at the candle-lit persecution complex
of a haunted sigh.

Amazing and convincing exile
on our way to fragility

The grimace of a latent maestro
pentagonal beggar
to allure the boundless treasure of eloquence
to cajole the heartless please of abstinence

Sometime

Nowhere

Will the rushing wind
waft the scent of our heartache
through the dying air?

Sometime

Nowhere.

Anchored in the harbor of death
a two-edged argument
tried to protect its experimental assonance
hazily answering to the fluctuation of the sea mist
lost in frozen blood
arguing against a fetus

His or her gesticulating corpse
infatuated with cleverness
charily approached the cliff
and climbed
and felt

No dirge waiting on the rocks
                    Just a starving ebb tide.

Annoying birthmark
the sign of their sins

desirable
endlessly
swinging ajar

to an atrophied world
bewildered and expectant

extraneous to fortitude

Does the flame of love eternal love
always gutter
when didactic thoughts
blow nothing but bubbles
and wistfully touch
the insufferable souvenir of beauty?

Pianissimo
     Cowardly
          losing countenance

the dazzling exactness of death
praises countless and haunting memories
gives depravation a date

forcing constricted openings
aggravating cheek to cheek tumefactions
on the edge of a cunnilingus
covert act of passion
definitively falling apart
helpless
     lecherous
         suddenly listless
         and acquiescent

Shangri-La
for the faithful
     Only.

Ad infinitum
does not mean forever

Ad infinitum
means giving love a birch
accepting converse theories
depriving Mary Magdalena of fragrance
Forget-me-not on the path to the Mount of Olives

Ad infinitum
here and now
bludgeoned to death
demolished
propelled by baleful ambitions

wherein exultation lies
in spite of all his faults

for evermore.

Shock therapy
after hearing papers rustling and choosing the primrose
path

More hell more heat
Livid with anger fleeing angels

     faddy ones
     instead of winged things

They already started counting down
It is too late
It is always too late

Rainmakers belong to dying away realities

Hailstorms are the one and only realities.

Amidships
on the doorsteps of dualism
failure eviscerates a shooting star
before throwing aside all restraint

Beware of the May queen my dear
Don't believe her careless whispers
at the time she becomes demented

Lament the fierceness of her tone
Unbosom yourself to the bumptious harridan

Leave your indifference on the shoreline
and gather the crying sunfishes
                         Anxiously.

Is fast love the ultimate accolade
in the deepness of your puzzled voice?

Does your flight dread the enigma
of lacerated butterflies?

The wanness of an antique disdain
The tenacity of delusions of grandeur

Admirable lament
on the eve of a terrible and arcane glory day
spinning the wheel again and again
to borrow the jarring note of marriage

Complacent billows of smoke
Deafening contraception
decaying inside the unadorned truth
                    Derelict.

To bet on the trusted
the only one

To gaze at the blood-red sins
openly

       bestial combat
       between dark distinctness
       and initial autonomy

To reappear
now
backbiting anguish
again always the same
       same words
       same feelings

The same PAIN

Is it so difficult to understand
that raw word?

PAIN

Why does love always snake
before finding its way to suffering hearts
while hate hits its target in the heart
and denudes the blessings from their truth?

Cadaverous cant phrases
mines
branded ones

Let my disquiet capitulate
be lenient towards my weirdness

Take the manacles away
but keep them
we never know

Marbled wrists sometimes
are a proof of love
lifelessly love.

Majestic sailboats
forever on the loose

are they meant to honour
the dowdiness of rococo waves?

They scintillate to avenge excision

They fulminate against the fanatic

Sharp anal shiver
encrusted with awkward barbarity

Bashful lovers
between Scylla and Charybdis

the perverse effect of edginess
the blind perfume of effeminacy

and dashingly handsome doubts
that brashly shine
for the last time
before breathing out.

A luminous desire
darkens the pavement
where he tried to blaze a trail

Boyish charm confers everlasting trouble
on decaying angels
who shared the brouhaha of the seraglio
where former lovers are still waiting
before they lose their exquisiteness
before they go into banishment

There is no excuse to calculated windings
to blithe attitudes

A brambly heart is not a heart
It brightens the colours of running tears
from the changeless heart

Stolid complicity
twisty retraction
Let the shimmering river mix feelings
take it all to the crude nowhere of love

Whimsically.

That bitter sense of the irrevocable
binds your soul to the incoherence
of titanic turnabouts

sarcastically
anxious to finish its crime
to quit the effect of erosion

mezzo forte attack
in the middle of nowhere
in the heart of the heart

providential concerto
in a sliding confidential mood

on the surface of dramatic pleasure

a last dress-run
before weeping over unbearable domination.

Can a simple departure
lacerate active imagination?

Red is not the colour of blood

Wake up and try
to encircle the lack of exaggeration
to catch at axiomatic formalism

Emend the certified brindled letters
the allopathic decrees

Go to hell
Boycott earthy conquest
and far-seeing disdain

Put yourself athwart the cavalcade of cheap survival
and sorrowful agitation

Don't leave for an impassive crusade
Stay with me. Here. Now.
On the foreland of our impossible love.

Let's dance on the carrousel of fame
        dark-eyed lover
and never repent
of fastening up the dress
and hiding the décolleté of your secrets

Someday some arid day
the necklace of pride will adorn it

Shall I be your pearl oyster?
Or will you prefer the plethora of cheap latex jewels?

Enamel hollow that conceals
the crannies of an almost broken heart

Austerity baffles the imagination of curved acuteness
but never assents to assiduous foreigners' bravado
never accepts prolific knights' braggadocio

In which foreword is it written
that courage should feel
its curiosity
awakened by a melancholy expression?

Eighteen weathercocks
Were singing on the roof of expensive despair
while a distrusted scar
declared itself taboo
draped in conjugal mistrust

a forceful argument
to hide baseless decency
to win restless fame

Applaud! Now and for never
Look askance at logical bows
the final ones

Prosaic minds
Orpheus come back from hell
Please
please me
arrow the downing day of coronation
beautify the battles of contrition

The echo of charming cocaine
with a scepter in her hand
loves the funeral solemnity
of the forever opposite bank

Is it faith in the unseen
or the look from a different corner
that drearily tells the conspirators
to follow the inaudibly attempt to stop the carnage decked
out in all his finery
and bluntly asking for the end of musical bondage?

He did it on purpose
but not alone

The resigned sadness of her elfin glance
the lack of bright imagination
the integrity of her pride
were no relief

He sat on the trunk of a fallen tree
and threw opal petals to the starving sky
to the starving love
the never started love

Chronic liar looking for a dissolute Cinderella
for the delicious scent of a downy forbidden fruit

Could he ever confess
his contradictory and frangible inclination
without gambling
casting a basilisk stare
at the spider web of defeat?

Boastfully?

He did.

With assumed nonchalance
and self-confidence made up of artificial airs  he
whimsically smiled at his own empty coffin

It returned his smile
without speaking
without offending the high aspirations of his beseeching
soul

He repented

The thin ascetic face he saw in the mirror of abandon
haunted the overshadowed body bag

triumphantly happy
to deliver him from falling
into that mean temptation

It did not kill him
It just let it die
          Flawlessly.

Exceedingly
        breakables

breaking loose
from evil-smelling ties

defensive ones
clumsy demotion
with a sprinkle of tenuous and savage resistance

felled in the ullage of gallantry

drunken cuddles

hocus-pocus
here is the bagpipe player
inveighing bounden duty against the harem of lonely
sheep
to create new evils
to extinguish the drowsy hope
and breastfeed the ambrosial charade
before sliding downwards in an eventual nightmare

Abduction from the seraglio.

A waxen and bug-eyed Cleopatra
empress of the whooper swans

circumspect
suffering a waste of civil wars
to defend cherubic queens

There comes the springtide
the diva
walking in high dudgeon
on  the crowded swamps
full of condescending toads

cultivated minds which do not care
avoiding infightings
and banning bigamous princes
who artfully deny
the sound of their footstep on the deck.

Legerdemain

                    the horizon disappeared
                    in a labyrinthine formula
                    and realized by some unmistakable sign
                    that the pyramids delivered
                    their oldest nonexistent maps
                    on some outworn papyrus

Who put the picture of a tsarina on that back issue?

Election to say never
            curtly
to bridge the gap between two sorrows
on the chessboard of surrealism

No unsafe choice
No disarming style

tritely nodding to conjugal fracture
                    to continual autocracy

There is something wonderfully honest
in that dried heart

            hitherto

grudgingly announcing the closure of hope

to immunize itself against any trace of love
to bury the burden
struggling under adamant caresses
running aground in the oasis of pain.